KIPLING

RUDYARD KIPLING
1865-1936

AN INTRODUCTION

GEOFF HUTCHINSON

Illustrations by Paul and Andy James

Contents

Introduction	*page* 3
The Kipling family	5
As a child in India	6
An English nightmare	8
Happier days	11
And so to school	12
India — The journalist	14
Success and marriage	18
Vermont	20
National figure — Fame and tragedy	22
The Boer War	24
Batemans	25
The final years	29
Summary	31

Acknowledgements

This booklet on the life and times of Rudyard Kipling is intended purely as an introduction, which I hope will encourage further study.

My thanks to Margaret Van Drat for the idea, Keith Fitz-Hugh for his patience, Paul and Andy James for the illustrations, Steve Nock of Dexterity Design Studio and Terry Dalton of Fastprint Ltd for use of materials and equipment, Jan Roadnight for her encouragement, and John Clegg for the inspiration gained from his excellent one-man show, *The Eye of the Sun.*

Special thanks also to the administrator and staff of Batemans, for their interest.

Geoff Hutchinson

Introduction

Half a mile to the south of the village of Burwash in East Sussex, down a narrow winding lane, stands the magnificent Jacobean sandstone mansion named Batemans.

Formerly a Sussex ironmaster's residence and built in 1634, it sits alone in the valley, surrounded by the rolling Sussex hills and was, between the years 1902 to 1936, the home of the celebrated author, Rudyard Kipling.

Born in India in 1865, Kipling was to become one of the most widely read and respected authors of his day, a national figure, much loved by millions for his imaginative creative writing.

It was at Batemans he spent the last 34 years of his life and achieved much recognition for some of his finest work, but his earlier life was equally, if not more, successful.

However, during his eventful life, from his early days in India to his final years at Batemans, Kipling experienced every emotion, and mingled with his successes were times of great anguish and tragedy.

The story of Rudyard Kipling . . .

The Kipling Family

The origins of the Kipling family lie in the county of Yorkshire.

Rudyard Kipling's father, John Lockwood Kipling (always known as Lockwood) was the eldest son of a Wesleyan minister, the Reverend Joseph and Frances Kipling and was born in Pickering in 1837. Lockwood attended school at Woodhouse Grove, and at the age of 22 was apprenticed to the Burslem potteries in Staffordshire as a modeller and designer. He was a very skilful man, who was to fulfil his great potential as a sculptor, artist and illustrator. He was also a most capable writer.

He soon left the potteries to work in an artist's studio and was then appointed to the staff of the executive art department of the South Kensington Museum in London. His father died at Skipton in 1862 and his mother survived until 1886 (Rudyard Kipling's 'Skipton grandmother' of whom he was to have clear recollection and fond memories).

Eventually, Lockwood met and courted a girl named Alice Macdonald. Alice was the same age as Lockwood and the daughter of a well-known Wesleyan preacher, George Browne Macdonald. She was of Scottish descent and came from a family of 11 children.

Three of her younger sisters eventually married into respectable families. Georgiana to Edward Burne-Jones, the eminent painter; Louisa to the industrialist, Alfred Baldwin, a marriage which was to produce the future Prime Minister, Stanley Baldwin; and Agnes to the artist, Edward Poynter.

Lockwood and Alice became engaged and were married at St Mary Abbots Church, Kensington on March 18th, 1865.

Earlier in 1865 Lockwood had been appointed to a post in a newly-formed school of art in Bombay, and less than a month after the wedding the couple had sailed for India. They arrived in the month of May.

On December 30th that year, after an agonisingly difficult confinement, Joseph Rudyard Kipling was born in Bombay.

As a Child in India

Geographically, India has not always been as we know it today. In 1865 its boundaries swallowed up the countries we now recognise as Pakistan, Bangladesh and the lower half of Burma. It was very much a part of the British Empire and Britain was almost totally responsible for its administration.

In common with other Victorian families living in India, the Kiplings were able to enjoy the accepted convenience of servants. Servant labour was plentiful and inexpensive.

Joseph Rudyard Kipling was baptised at Bombay Cathedral. The first christian name was never used and the second (a commemoration of his parents' visit to Rudyard Lake, near Leek in Staffordshire), often shortened to Ruddy or Rud, was the name he would use throughout his life.

The young Rudyard was looked after by an ayah (a nanny) and had at his command domestic helpers of all kinds. Surrounded by these native servants who unquestioningly answered his call, it was inconceivable to Rudyard that anyone should disobey his wishes, and this caused him to be an exceptionally spoilt, highly strung child. He had a mind of his own, was prone to screaming tantrums when disciplined and was extremely difficult to control.

Rudyard's birth had nearly caused the death of his mother and when she became pregnant again in 1867, she was advised on medical grounds to return to England where the birth could take place under better conditions. This advice was heeded and she took the two-and-a-half year old Rudyard to her parents' home in the village of Bewdley, on the River Severn. The grandparents were distressed by the disturbing effect the unruly Rudyard had on their normally quiet routine. His grandmother unhappily declared that he was a problem and capable of upsetting any household. She hoped his father would take a firmer line with him when the family returned to India.

After another dangerous confinement, a daughter, Alice, was born in June of 1868. Due to her mother's description of her as a 'tricksy baby', Alice became known to all the family as Trixie or Trix. When she was five months old they returned to Bombay and the family lived there together for a further three years.

Always in the presence of his Indian servant minders, Rudyard soon began to learn their Hindustani dialect and used it constantly as his only means of communication. He was often reminded by his parents to speak English when addressing them.

Accompanied by servants, the young Rudyard was taken to many places white adults would never go; the Hindu temples, the bazaars and food markets and it all made lasting impressions on him, impressions which were to emerge in later years as he expressed these early childhood recollections in his writing.

The only blot on the Kipling family's otherwise happy and uncomplicated life in India was the death of a newborn baby son, in 1870.

But the happiness was not to last for Rudyard and in 1871, approaching the age of six, he was about to embark on one of the most traumatic periods of his young life.

An English Nightmare

In the year 1871, Lockwood and Alice Kipling made a decision, which to us now may seem a little strange.

The Indian hot season was approaching, and the heat of Bombay during this period brought the increased risk of infection and disease, making it a particularly dangerous place for European children.

It had been the practice in previous seasons for the children to be taken into the cooler regions in the hills surrounding the city, but this year alternative plans were made.

It was common and accepted procedure for families in England to specialise in fostering the children of working people in India and to provide them with a limited form of education. These services were often advertised in the Indian press, and it was through one of these advertisements that arrangements were made to send Rudyard and Trix to England.

Although the Kiplings' relatives in England were aware of the situation and would have almost certainly accommodated the youngsters, Lockwood and Alice, for reasons known only to themselves, decided to send their two children, Rudyard, aged five-and-a-half and Trix, nearly three, to the residence of the Holloway family in Southsea. The Kiplings did not know the Holloways but satisfactory references must have been supplied and they readily agreed to place the children in their care.

The reasoning behind the Kiplings' thinking has been much discussed. Rudyard, as previously stated, was an undisciplined young lad and perhaps they thought his disorderly behaviour could be checked if he were to be placed with strangers and away from relatives, where he may well have become yet more spoilt. Perhaps it was a feeling they wished to remain independent. Whatever the reasons, undoubtedly the cruellest part of this episode was the way the parents kept their children totally ignorant of their plans and gave no explanation for the sudden desertion.

On April 15th, 1871, accompanied by their mother, the children boarded the P&O paddlesteamer *Ripon* for the voyage to England.

They were taken to the suburbs of Southsea to a house called Lorne Lodge, a damp, dismal, unwelcoming place, which was to be their home for the next five years.

They were placed in the care of Mr and Mrs Holloway, 'Aunty Rosa' and 'Uncle Harry' as they were to be known to the children. Mr Holloway was a retired naval man. He took a liking to the children and was a companion for Rudyard. He was a fair-minded man and Rudyard had made a friend.

His wife, however, was quite the reverse. She was a harsh, dominant disciplinarian. Her word was final! She was a deeply religious woman, who administered her discipline with harsh evangelical passion.

The couple had a hateful 12-year-old son, Harry, who was adored by his mother. He could do no wrong in her eyes! It was Rudyard's misfortune to share an attic room with Harry, who professed the same religious fervour as his mother, but who proved to be no more than a cruel and evil bully, a tormentor to both children. Rudyard referred to him as 'Devil Boy'.

To make the situation worse Mrs Holloway, who had always wanted a daughter, made a pet of Trix and vented her full wrath on Rudyard. Many times he was punished for trivial offences and many times he was beaten.

The children were given a form of basic education. Mrs Holloway held lessons around the dining room table and taught the children to read together. Rudyard was a slow learner. His sister was able to read before him and he did not master the art until he was seven years old. He did, however, quickly improve.

Rudyard's friendship with the mild-mannered, fair-minded 'Uncle Harry', his one crumb of comfort in this unhappy house, was unfortunately not to last. Mr Holloway died in 1874, after 2½ years of the children's stay, and from this point on, what little protection Rudyard could count on was taken away and the punishments increased in their frequency and severity.

Although they eventually wrote regularly to Bombay, neither child could tell their parents of their unhappiness, as their letters were strictly censored by the harrowing Mrs Holloway. The fear of further punishment was a strong enough deterrent.

For one month each year Rudyard spent his Christmas holidays with his Aunt Georgie Burne-Jones at The Grange, North End Road in Fulham, and these visits were pleasurable interludes away from the place Rudyard termed 'The House of Desolation'.

During his spell at Lorne Lodge, Rudyard's eyesight deteriorated. He suffered from extreme short sight and strong spectacles were recommended.

Although this time at Southsea was a miserable part of his life, Rudyard stuck at it with a resigned acceptance, and it would appear it was not to have too harmful an effect on his future development.

It must be stated that when he first came to Lorne Lodge he was a spoilt, undisciplined boy and although the methods used by Mrs Holloway could not be condoned, perhaps there were many times when his punishment was thoroughly deserved. That he suffered there is no doubt.

The more mature boy who left 'The House of Desolation' was far removed from the unruly child who had arrived five years earlier.

HAPPIER DAYS

It was in March 1877 that Mrs Kipling took the children away from Lorne Lodge. The nightmare was over. Rudyard had only the slightest recollection of his mother and Trix did not remember her at all.

Mrs Kipling had decided the children needed a change from the discipline of Southsea and she felt the time had come to rebuild her relationship with them, to get to know them again.

That summer was spent at a farmhouse, on the edge of Epping Forest. The children were given small tasks to perform around the farm and were generally given free run of the place. Their cousin, nine-year-old Stanley Baldwin, was a visitor and the two boys got on well together, indulging in many a mischievous prank. This countryside adventure was a delightful new experience for Rudyard and Trix, much divorced from the agonies of Lorne Lodge.

After leaving the farm, the family took lodgings at 227 Brompton Road. Rudyard found London a fascinating place with much to see and explore. He and his sister spent many happy hours at the museums in Kensington, and generally their time in the capital was a rewarding and enjoyable experience.

However, it was now that Rudyard first experienced a condition which would stay with him all his life — insomnia. Many nights the 12-year-old would wander the house, unable to switch his mind off, and incapable of falling asleep.

This apart, Rudyard found his time in London an ideal remedy for erasing the sad memories he held of his days at Southsea.

Later in the year his mother returned to India and Rudyard and Trix were placed in the care of three ladies, Mrs Winnard, and the sisters Mary and Georgina Craik, who lived in Kensington High Street. The household had a pleasant, kindly atmosphere and it was here that Rudyard would spend his school holidays during the next few years.

And So To School

In 1878 the time had come for Rudyard Kipling to begin his formal education. The decision was made to place him at the United Services College, an experimental establishment in the Devonshire resort of Westward Ho!. The headmaster of the school, Cormell Price, was a family friend and was already known to Rudyard as 'Uncle Crom'. In January 1878 Rudyard made his first attendance.

The United Services College had been founded in 1874 by a group of retired Army and Navy officers with the intention of running it on public school lines, but without exhorbitant fees. Most of the boys in attendance were the sons of army officers, who were destined to follow in their fathers' footsteps. Others had the same circumstances as Rudyard with parents living in India and a strong Anglo-Indian atmosphere prevailed.

Despite its military-style title and its objective of passing boys onto the army, the school was surprisingly free from militarism in its curriculum. There were few military trappings, the school providing its pupils with a general education in all subjects. There was also no great emphasis on religion, as was the case with many Victorian schools. Cormell Price was not a committed Christian and his views seemed reflected in the attitude of the establishment. There was a chaplain, but no chapel and prayers were held in a communal all-purpose hall.

The school buildings comprised of 12 bleak houses joined together as one long terrace. The discipline at the school was severe, the food uninspiring and in common with many Victorian public schools, there was an element of bullying towards the new entrants.

Kipling described his first term as 'horrible', his time spent dodging the bullies and the cane-swinging chaplain, Mr Campbell.

After this first, rather problematic term, Rudyard was looking forward to a visit from his parents for the Easter holidays, but they were unable to come and he was forced to spend his holiday at the school. This, however, was not as unpleasant as he imagined it would be. The school was a different place out of term time when most of the boys had gone and Rudyard found it a great improvement and quite enjoyable. After that rather trying first term, he settled into his school life with enthusiasm and determination. He became unaffected by the bullying and his schoolwork progressed from strength to strength. Further improvement came after Rudyard's second year, when the sadistic chaplain was replaced by the milder-mannered Reverend Willes.

Due to his shortsightedness, Kipling was unable to participate in sporting activities, but it did not stop him being an avid reader and he studied the works of Tennyson, Browning, Swinburne, Thackeray, Dickens, Bunyan and Defoe. Longfellow was a favourite and he loved the poems of Emerson and the words of Mark Twain. He became known in the school as an authority on literary matters. He was the only boy in the school to wear spectacles and was given the nickname 'Giggers'.

Rudyard teamed up with two of his colleagues at the school, L. C. Dunsterville and George Beresford, and the three became good friends, sharing a room and embarking on their schoolboy escapades together. The three friends were later to be represented in *Stalky and Co*, a work of fiction very loosely based on Kipling's time at Westward Ho!.

The headmaster was very impressed with Kipling's progress at the school. He was convinced by 1880 that Rudyard would become a writer and in 1881 appointed him to the editorship of the school newspaper *The United Services College Chronicle*, a position Kipling held for his last two years at the school.

During 1881 he considered becoming a doctor, but the idea soon passed and in his last term at the school in 1882 he was totally committed to writing. He sent his work to the 'dear old ladies' of Kensington, for criticism and also sent his parents collections of poetry. Unbeknown to him, in 1881, driven by parental pride in their son's ability, Lockwood and Alice had this poetry printed in India under the title *Schoolboy Lyrics*.

At the age of 16, his formal education finished, the time had come to move on to the next stage of his eventful life . . . a return to India.

Kipling now exuded a maturity beyond his 16 years and his physical appearance led many to think he was in his early twenties.

During his time at the college, he had had his first serious (for him) encounter with the opposite sex, when during school holidays he had met 15-year-old Florence Garrard. Just 14 years old himself, he was much attracted to her. They met regularly and before returning to India he suggested they become engaged, but two years later she wrote to break it off. In the spring of 1890 he was to meet her in London, where they briefly resumed their relationship, before she rejected him completely. Florence was later to appear as Masie in Kipling's first novel, *The Light That Failed*.

INDIA — THE JOURNALIST

Lockwood Kipling would ideally have liked his son to have continued his education at Oxford. Impressed by Rudyard's promising literary talents it was something he felt would have enhanced his son's progress. But it was not to be. Kipling senior was unable to afford the fees, and as an alternative he secured a job for Rudyard in India working on an English newspaper in Lahore, *The Civil and Military Gazette.* He would be paid around 150 rupees per month.

At first Rudyard was unhappy with this arrangement. He felt as a writer his future should be in England, but eventually accepting his father's decision, he sailed for India, arriving in Bombay in October 1882. From Bombay he travelled by train the 1,000 miles to Lahore in the north-west of the country to stay with his parents.

The Civil and Military Gazette had the biggest circulation in the Punjab. It had a large native staff and an English editor, Stephen Wheeler.

Work for the 17-year-old cub reporter was hard. Rudyard was thrown into the deep end by his demanding, uncompromising editor. He never worked less than 10 hours a day and some days even longer. Matured far beyond his years Kipling found his challenging job a stimulating experience. Due to his editor's frequent bouts of fever, he was often left to run the paper alone, a daunting task for one so young, however mature. But Kipling coped well. Despite the intense heat and constant threat of fever, he loved India and its people and his profession enabled him to build up his knowledge of the country. Sometimes late at night when the paper had gone to press, unable to sleep, he would wander the mysterious streets of Lahore, drinking in its unique atmosphere.

He eventually became a member of the Punjab Club, where he would take his meals and meet people from all walks of Indian administrational life, civil servants, army officers and the like. He listened intently to their conversations . . . and learned. He also mingled with the native population. He was ever eager for the story, the scandal, the gossip, all the time gaining fresh experience.

Through his meetings with military personnel during this period, the seeds of his lifelong admiration and devotion to the army were sown.

Unable to serve due to his short sight, Kipling delighted in these military contacts, reporting on life in the army from the Officers' Mess to the lowest ranks. He had a great sympathy for the ordinary private soldier and sought to improve his lot. He developed a preference for the man of action as against the politicians and thinkers. He considered his proudest moment in India to be when the Army Commander-in-Chief consulted him about the true feelings among the rank and file.

Kipling was a small, dynamic young man. Standing just five feet six inches tall, he walked upright with a quick, purposeful stride — a bundle of energy. He was a great conversationalist, frequently using his hands to emphasise a point he was making. He was never stuck for something to say and he was an even better listener. His enthusiastic approach to journalism sometimes caused offence. Many thought him lacking in manners and his sometimes over-zealous methods made him less than popular in certain circles.

In the later part of 1883, Kipling was left alone at his parents' house while his father was away on business and his mother was in England. He was not happy with this arrangement, but it was soon forgotten when his mother brought his sister back from England. Trix was now 15 years old and the family had become a complete unit once more, a situation which gave Rudyard great satisfaction.

In 1885 Kipling became a freemason when he joined the Lahore Lodge, and from 1886, with the *Gazette* under new editorship, he began to produce weekly pieces on important local issues and was also allowed to use his poetry as fillers in the paper when editorial content fell short. A collection of these poems was published anonymously in a limited edition of 350 copies and it sold out fast. A second edition was published, this time under his name and was given the title *Departmental Ditties.* It was a collection of titillating, mildly shocking, snippets of Anglo-Indian life and it proved very popular. By 1886 the name of Kipling was known across the Indian continent.

In 1887 he was promoted to the staff of the *Gazette's* sister paper the *Pioneer,* and it involved him travelling half way across India to take up his post at Allahabad, a city with a large Hindu population.

The job meant more responsibility, with a weekly supplement to edit. He entered into the job with his usual enthusiasm and welcomed the chance to explore a new Indian city.

In January 1888 Kipling's first book of fiction was published under the title *Plain Tales from the Hills.* It was a portrait of Anglo-Indian life and

most of the 40 tales had app
The book was enormously
sold out.

While in Allahabad he befr
and his wife Edmonia and i
with them. During this tim
Sheep, a short story based o
Lorne Lodge. Kipling later
with Mrs Hill's sister, Caroli
of the affair.

The stories he wrote for th
published in successive paper
Library, bringing him yet n

Later in 1889 his sister T
Fleming, a soldier in th
Kipling was not p
He had other plans

India — Kipling's inspiration

earlier in the *Gazette*.
ar in India and soon

d Professor Aleck Hill
1888 he went to stay
wrote *Baa Baa Black*
unhappy memories of
ed a romantic liaison
t nothing serious came

eer were collected and
by the Indian Railway
valued revenue.

vas married to John
vey Department, but
at the wedding.

His success in India as a writer had made him even more determined that he should return to London, the centre of the English-speaking literary world, and with money he had gained from the sales of his books, he was able to take a leisurely return. Still only 23 years of age, he decided to depart.

He was to return to India just once more but his main association with the country was over. His time in India had been an immensely happy one and his knowledge and lasting impressions gained from his extensive travels in this massive continent were to surface later in some of his greatest works.

His years in India had done much to shape his beliefs and determine his political leanings. Kipling was an imperialist who believed countries required firm government for their own benefit and who better to govern, he thought, than the British, whom he considered did the job well. He believed the British Empire to be the only acceptable administration.

He thought the civilised English-speaking nations, 'the white man', better qualified to command not because of colour but because of superior past achievements, better resources and organisation.

He respected the rights and customs of other races and considered them to be excellent at many things, but he genuinely believed it was 'the white man's' duty to govern. Later, in 1899, these opinions were forcibly expressed in the poem *The White Man's Burden*.

Not surprisingly, his views were often misunderstood.

SUCCESS AND MARRIAGE

In March 1889 Kipling sailed from Calcutta and during his unhurried return to England he made brief visits to Burma, Singapore, Hong Kong and China. He also spent a month in Japan and then moved on to San Francisco. After visiting Canada (a country which much impressed him), he returned once more to the United States, where he finally sailed for England and arrived in London in October 1889.

He took rooms in Villiers Street, adjacent to Charing Cross railway station, made new literary contacts, joined the Savile Club, and was soon actively engaged at writing in his new surroundings. His books were now being published, and selling well in England. He was a success and his fame was growing rapidly.

However, he found certain aspects of London depressing. He disliked the decadence of London society of the 1890s and he detested the behaviour of fashionable writers such as Oscar Wilde.

Although having a close circle of friends, Kipling's engrossment in his work made him a very lonely man. He suffered frequently from periods of depression and began to miss the warmth of the Indian sun. Also, it was while in residence in Villiers Street, he resumed his previously-mentioned ill-fated affair with Flo Garrard.

Nevertheless, the year 1890 was a momentous one for the 24-year-old writer. Apart from the success of his books, he was contributing to several quality magazines and periodicals.

Plain Tales from the Hills and *The Light That Failed* were selling fast and his Indian Railway Library stories were published in collections entitled *Soldiers Three* and *Wee Willie Winkie.*

This year also saw the appearance in periodicals of the enormously successful *Barrack-Room Ballads,* poems depicting the life of the ordinary British soldier serving in India. They included the haunting *Danny Deever* and *Mandalay.* Two years later the ballads were published in book form and by the end of the century they were being recited and sung widely in the music-halls of England.

Kipling's fame continued to spread and by 1891 he was a household name in both England and America.

Soon after arriving in London Kipling had met a young American writer named Wolcott Balestier. Balestier was eager to collaborate with an English author to write a novel and Kipling soon became his target. The two became great friends, possibly Kipling's closest friendship. Together they wrote the novel *The Naulahka* (fabulous jewel), and it was eventually published in 1892.

In 1890 Kipling was introduced to Wolcott's sister Caroline, while she was visiting England with her mother and sister. She was three years his senior, small, energetic and lively and he found her most attractive. He courted her but no immediate plans were made to marry.

That winter Kipling became ill. Malaria and dysentery contracted in India, coupled to exhaustion through overwork, had laid him low and he was advised that a long sea voyage might help to improve his health. In August 1891 he set off round the world alone.

He made brief visits to South Africa, New Zealand and Australia and late in the year he landed in Ceylon, now known as Sri Lanka, and took a train through India to Lahore to visit his parents.

During his stay he received a cable from Caroline saying her brother Wolcott had died of typhoid while visiting Germany. Shocked and distressed at the loss of his friend, he left at once to return to England to comfort the family. He arrived back in England on January 10th, 1892.

United stronger by their shared grief, Kipling proposed to Caroline and they were married on January 18th, 1892 at All Souls Church, Langham Place, in London.

It was a quiet wedding with only four guests in attendance, and the bride was given away by the American author, Henry James.

Vermont

With his continuing success as a writer, Kipling was becoming financially very sound and the lack of monetary worries prompted him to take his 'Carrie' honeymooning on a round the world trip.

The couple landed in New York in the February of 1892, and quickly moved north to visit Carrie's family in Brattleboro, Vermont.

The time spent there was pleasurable, so much so that plans were made for them to eventually settle. Kipling was well liked by Carrie's family and her brother Beatty arranged for a piece of land to be made available on which they would later build their own home. Rudyard and Carrie continued their journey by travelling to the west of the continent by way of Canada and on to Japan. While in Japan, Kipling had deposited a large sum of money into the New Oriental Bank, but when attempting to make a withdrawal he was informed the bank had crashed. Their money gone, the Kiplings had to make a hasty retreat to Vermont.

Rudyard and Carrie lived modestly at Brattleboro for a year in a small dwelling on the estate, Bliss Cottage, paying a monthly rent of £2. In late December 1892 their first child, Josephine, was born, and in the following spring the building work started for their new home. They occupied the house in late summer. It was named Naulakha (the correct spelling; the book title was wrong and why Kipling did not correct it remains a mystery), in memory of Wolcott Balestier, and was to be their home for the next three years. They were happy, productive years for Kipling as he wrote his stories and poetry based on his previous experiences in India — *The Jungle Book, The Second Jungle Book* and the collected stories of *Many Inventions.* All proved hugely successful.

The Kiplings journeyed to Bermuda and in 1895 returned to England to visit Rudyard's parents who were now living in Wiltshire.

In February 1896 their second child, Elsie was born.

During this period in America, a rather odd obsession began to take root. Kipling developed a fear of intrusion into his private life, especially by the popular newspapers. For one so famous he seemed rather naive to expect indifference from pressmen. He had once been glad of their glowing reviews. Nevertheless, he considered it was not part of his public life to be interviewed. He began to be obstructive to journalists, and his relationship with the press deteriorated rapidly.

Apart from this the years spent in Vermont were among the happiest of his life. Surrounded by his young family Kipling was a fulfilled man. He took great interest in the countryside, wildlife and the seasons and even contemplated becoming a naturalised American. He adored his children. He loved to entertain them with his stories and his books for youngsters reflect the deep affection he held for all children.

Unfortunately the happiness was not to last as events were to take a vicious turn to upset the orderly existence. In 1895 the United States and Britain were entangled in a political dispute over frontiers in South America. The two countries were exchanging bitter words and at one point war seemed a possibility, but eventually matters were resolved peacefully. Kipling felt a certain air of suspicion and antagonism towards him and, quite understandably, it gave him a feeling of unease. He no longer felt comfortable being an Englishman in America. But a more serious threat to his future happiness in Vermont materialised when he became embroiled in a family disagreement with his brother-in-law.

Beatty Balestier had fallen on hard times. He was bankrupt, had resorted to heavy drinking and was regarded as a total failure. Kipling's fame and financial standing aggravated the situation and Beatty was consumed by envy. He became aggressive towards Kipling and in a drunken rage he threatened to kill him. Whether the threat was serious or not, it frightened Kipling enough to rather misguidedly report the matter to the police.

For a man who disliked intrusion into his private life, it was certainly the worst decision he could have made. Newsmen from all parts, irritated by Kipling's attitude towards them, descended on Brattleboro to report the initial hearing on May 12th, 1896 . . . to bait their prey and exaggerate their stories.

The defence lawyers claimed Kipling was making a mountain from a molehill and that he had indeed been in too much haste to report what they considered just a family tiff. Kipling now had to endure the full glare of this unwanted publicity.

The hearing was adjourned, a trial set for September and Beatty was given bail. The whole affair had temporarily flattened Kipling. He decided there and then he could not recapture the happy times at Vermont and the family decided to return to England before the trial took place.

They left Vermont with much reluctance and a great sadness.

NATIONAL FIGURE – FAME AND TRAGEDY

The Kiplings arrived back in England in September 1896 and took residence in Maidencombe, near Torquay. The following year they moved to the village of Rottingdean, near Brighton in Sussex, where they lived for a short while at 'North End House', the summer residence of the Burne-Joneses. During this time a son, John, was born in August 1897. In September they made the short move across the village green to 'The Elms' and this was their home for the next five years.

Kipling began to contribute a series of poems to *The Times* newspaper commenting on significant issues of the day, sobering words warning of the perils facing the country. The best known of these poems, *Recessional,* written for Queen Victoria's Golden Jubilee in 1897, warned of the irresponsible use of power. The poems created wide interest and comment. Kipling had become a national figure.

He also expressed the opinion that Britain should not sit back and wait for war, but should defend herself by exertion. He was often misunderstood, many dismissed him as a warmonger, but sadly, many of his predictions were to come true.

The novel, *Captains Courageous,* was published in 1897 and the following year a collection of stories under the title *A Day's Work* appeared. At the beginning of 1897, Kipling received a visit from an American publisher named Frank N. Doubleday. The Kiplings had met him two years previously in Vermont and he became a great friend, known affectionately by his initials, 'Effendi'. Doubleday published all the American editions of Kipling's works.

In January of 1898 the family sailed for Cape Town to avoid the English winter and to take a second look at a country Rudyard had visited earlier in his life.

During this visit Kipling met Cecil Rhodes, the founder of Rhodesia, a man whose achievements he much admired and the two men became friends. Two years later Rhodes was to build a house for Kipling on the

Groote Schuur estate. The dwelling was named The Woolsack and the Kiplings returned there most winters until 1907.

Kipling's visit to southern Africa in 1898 included a train journey from South Africa into Rhodesia to Bulawayo, where he explored the surrounding countryside on a bicycle. In South Africa he visited the Boer republics of the Transvaal and the Orange Free State. He studied the appalling living conditions of the English-speaking settlers who were living in these areas and was disturbed at what he saw. Their plight had a profound effect on his thinking. From this point on he became convinced the Boers were not to his liking and was determined to do all he could to improve the situation.

He left South Africa in April, 1898 fired with the intention of returning the following winter, but his plans had to be changed. Carrie wished to see her mother in Vermont and Kipling himself had more American copyright problems to sort out.

On the voyage across the Atlantic, sea conditions were rough. Josephine and Elsie both caught exceptionally bad colds and their health deteriorated still further when the family arrived in New York. After a few days they improved, but now it was Carrie's turn to be ill. She developed a fever, and finally Kipling himself was taken seriously ill with pneumonia.

His condition worsened and he was declared dangerously ill. The word spread of his illness and his many admirers waited anxiously for bulletins on the progress of the 33-year-old author. He eventually recovered, but this freakish spate of illnesses had a terrible sting in the tail.

His six-year-old daughter, Josephine had suffered a relapse. Two days after her father was declared out of danger, she died at 6am on March 6th, 1899. The Kiplings had lost a daughter they adored. It was a devastating blow.

It took Kipling many months to regain his health and it was not until the June of 1899 that he was considered fit to travel, when the sad party left for England.

Kipling never visited the United States of America again in his life.

The Boer War

The situation in South Africa had deteriorated during Kipling's illness and in October 1899 the South African War (The Boer War) broke out. Kipling solidly supported the British view and worked relentlessly for victory.

In England he formed fund-raising committees for the dependants of the soldiers. He wrote a poem entitled *The Absent Minded Beggar* and donated the proceeds. It was published by the *Daily Mail*, and the composer Sir Arthur Sullivan wrote music to it. The poem generated much interest and eventually a sum of over £250,000 was raised.

He visited South Africa many times during the course of the war and while there he did all he could to help the war effort. He visited the wounded, gave morale boosting speeches, worked for an army newspaper and was consulted by politicians and senior army personnel for his comments. On several occasions he came under fire while reporting from the battlefields. His patriotic fervour was running high.

Peace finally came in 1902, following Britain's hard won victory. Kipling was disappointed, not by Britain's triumph, but by what was to happen next. It was decided to set up the Union of South Africa, under the British Crown, giving equal rights to the Boers. Kipling disagreed strongly with this. He felt the Boers should always be viewed as the aggressors and he considered them an inferior race incapable of rational government. He applied the same beliefs he held over India, that the British were the only nation fit to provide a stable government. His inflexible views were not always popular.

He also expressed the view that the British army was not as efficient as he felt it might have been during the war. He was disappointed that soldiers were sent to the front ill-prepared for battle and it was a matter which troubled him and dwelt on his mind long after the war was over.

In 1902 he completed his *Just So Stories* for children in Cape Town and continued to visit South Africa until 1907.

BATEMANS

Kipling's disillusionment with the outcome of the South African War and the British unpreparedness continued to prey on his mind. He was determined to do all in his power to ensure things would be much different if Britain was required to fight again. He saw the early storm clouds of war gathering over Europe and gave frequent warnings of the growing German threat. He implored the nation to be aware and prepared.

So concerned was he over this military inefficiency he formed a club in Rottingdean to teach the young men of the area the art of rifle shooting, morse and semaphore. They were regularly drilled and given a basic military training. Kipling took the whole affair very seriously. The club eventually had a membership of over 30. Kipling sincerely believed his experiment should be repeated across the country and should be an essential part of a young man's upbringing.

The period 1899 till 1902 saw the publication of several of Kipling's more famous works. His schoolboy tale, *Stalky and Co* appeared in 1899 and in 1901 came what is regarded by many as his most accomplished work, and described as one of the greatest novels in the English language, *Kim.* Here he drew on his vast experience of India and *Kim* is considered to be the finest story ever derived from that country.

Kipling continued to spend much of his time in South Africa and before leaving England in 1901 he published a poem in *The Times* called *The Islanders.* It was a stinging broadside to the nation on his favourite theme, the British reluctance to devote their time to military preparedness. He mockingly implied that the country was too busy playing games such as football and cricket and neglecting its real duty. He suggested that Britain's comfortable lifestyle could only survive if it was prepared to fight for it. The poem caused great offence but Kipling was unperturbed.

While in South Africa, he was saddened to learn of the death of his friend, Cecil Rhodes. Kipling composed and read verses at a memorial service and on April 3rd, 1902 he attended the State funeral in Cape Town.

Back at Rottingdean, intrusion into his personal life was still uppermost in his mind. He took great exception to the sightseers who came to peer into his garden, and sometimes into his house. He complained bitterly to the bus companies who organised such trips. His complaints fell on deaf ears. Everyone wanted a glimpse of the great writer. It was extremely annoying for a man who preferred to meet people on his own terms. Also the loss of Josephine and the memory of her presence in 'The Elms' caused the Kiplings much heartache and was almost certainly a big factor in their decision to leave.

Soon the 36-year-old Kipling was to find a home which would very much give him the privacy and happiness he desired and which would be his home for the rest of his life.

Kipling was one of the earliest motoring enthusiasts in the country and for two years he and Carrie had travelled the length and breadth of Sussex in search of a new home. In 1900, on one of these househunting trips (this time by train, the car had broken down) they travelled to Burwash in the east of the county, where they discovered Batemans, a sandstone Jacobean house, built in 1634 and situated half a mile south of the village.

Batemans — Kipling's home for 34 years

They were both smitten with the place, but unfortunately for them the house was soon rented and they had missed their chance.

However, two years later they heard that Batemans was vacant again and this time swooped quickly to secure the purchase.

The house was bought for the sum of £9,300 and they moved in in early September, 1902.

By 1905 the adjoining Dudwell Mill and farm had been purchased, making a total area of 300 acres. Kipling had the waterwheel removed from the mill and installed a generator to provide electricity for the estate.

At Batemans Kipling now took his inspiration from the countryside of Sussex to produce some of his finest work. Now ensured of privacy and seclusion and with his ever-faithful Carrie keeping away unwanted visitors, his imagination ran wild. Many well-known works flowed from his pen in the first 10 years of his occupancy of Batemans; *Traffics and Discoveries* in 1904, *Puck of Pook's Hill* (1906), *Actions and Reactions* (1909) and *Rewards and Fairies* in 1910. Kipling was pleased with his efforts. He considered *Puck of Pook's Hill,* with its Batemans setting (the hill is visible to the south-west) and its sequel, *Rewards and Fairies* to be among the best works he had produced. The story *They,* with its ghostly children, reflecting his grief at the loss of his daughter, and the famous poem *If* were written during this period.

Carrie continued to manage his business affairs, a task she had performed admirably throughout the years and much entertaining was done at Batemans. It became a popular meeting place and Kipling was a fine host. His good friend, Rider Haggard, was among the long line of distinguished guests. Kipling still continued his travels. In 1907 he took a trip to Canada and visited Stockholm to proudly receive the Nobel Prize for Literature. Between 1909 and 1914 the family visited France for their winter holidays and in 1913 they ventured as far as Egypt.

Kipling's mother died in November 1910, quickly followed by his father, following a heart attack in January 1911. Kipling owed much to the encouragement and advice given by his father earlier in his career.

Also in 1910 he learned of the death of his ex-headmaster, Cormell Price. Kipling wrote the verse for the engraved tablet which stands beneath the stained glass window in Westward Ho! church, 'Who with toil of his today, Bought for us tomorrow'.

In 1913 Kipling appeared to be the obvious choice to fill the office of Poet Laureate, left vacant by the death of Alfred Austin, but he was not approached. Prime Minister Asquith was aware of Kipling's independent views and his intransigent reluctance to write to order, and thought it useless to ask him. The Laureateship was accepted by Robert Bridges.

Although Kipling had been for many years regarded as the poet of the people, it is almost certain he would have refused the post. Throughout his life many great honours, including a knighthood, were extended to him and each time he declined. He would accept no honour he felt would compromise him in any way. He believed he should always be free to write and say exactly what he felt. He reasoned that such honours were given by politicians and at the time they were offered, he did not wish to be obliged to any particular party. Even the Order of Merit, offered by the King and with no political significance, was twice refused. Kipling deemed it sufficient that the King of England should think so highly of him to make the offer, and while ensuring His Majesty of his undying loyalty, he politely refused acceptance. He did, however, accept honorary degrees, including one at Oxford in 1907.

In 1914 the war Kipling had prophesied so accurately became a reality and he and Carrie eagerly played their part in the war effort by aiding Belgian refugees and devoting time to helping the Red Cross. He was filled with great pride when his 17-year-old son, John, secured a commission with the Irish Guards and reported for duty in September 1914.

Although not a fit man, Kipling embarked on a tour of military hospitals and army camps in England and in August 1915 he visited the troops in the battlefields of France. He was also requested to visit Royal Navy ships and sound his patriotic call to the crews.

After returning to Batemans in 1915 he was given the news that his subaltern son was missing, presumed dead, in France. His body was never found and it was over two years before the tragic circumstances of his death were finally verified.

Kipling later wrote *The Irish Guards in the Great War*, which was published in 1923.

THE FINAL YEARS

Due to his many other commitments during the war years, Kipling's literary output was naturally much decreased.

After the war his ill health continued, but he was still able to travel extensively, many times to France when he was appointed a member of the Imperial War Graves Commission. On one such visit in 1922 he was presented to King George V and a lasting friendship was formed.

Kipling was a great celebrity, much in demand. In July 1924 he was granted the freedom of the City of London.

On October 22nd, 1924, his daughter, Elsie was married to Captain George Bambridge of the Irish Guards. Kipling had mixed feelings about the departure of his one remaining child.

His long journeys were not over either. He visited North Africa and achieved a life-long ambition when he visited Brazil in 1927. In 1930, at the age of 65, he went to the West Indies and this was his last long voyage.

He had now become an isolated figure politically, moving still further to the right. He held no allegiance to any particular party or group. He had little respect for his cousin Stanley Baldwin's political views, and described him as 'a socialist at heart'.

The loss of his son during the Great War had intensified his mistrust and hatred of Germany. It was a hatred that was never to diminish. He felt bitter and dejected at what he saw as lost opportunities following the war. He was depressed by the sickening loss of life and felt that those who had died had perished in vain, for he truly believed the Great War was not the war to end all wars and that the Germans were far from finished. He was to give early warnings of Hitler's aggressive intentions.

Still he continued to write and entertain at his beloved Batemans, but as his health deteriorated so his writing took on a more sombre, depressing tone. His final collection of stories appeared under the title *Limits and Renewals* in 1932 and was punctuated with references to disease, pain and madness.

In 1932 Kipling prepared a selection of verse and prose for the

American market under the title *A Pageant of Kipling* and also the vast Sussex Edition of his work in 35 volumes. At the end of the year his gross income was over £32,000.

By now Carrie's health was almost as bad as her husband's. She had become diabetic, she suffered from acute rheumatism and later developed gout.

The following years were to be filled with pain and an increasing feeling of loneliness and isolation. Kipling had been ill on and off since 1915, suffering from gastritis and in 1933 it was diagnosed he was suffering from duodenal ulcers.

At the beginning of 1936 the Kiplings planned to visit Cannes. Before they had left the country the 70-year-old Kipling was taken ill with a haemorrhage and taken to the Middlesex Hospital, where he died on January 18th 1936, the 44th anniversary of his marriage to Caroline. He was cremated at Golders Green on January 20th. The same day his friend, King George V, had passed away at Sandringham.

The Prime Minister was among the pall bearers as Kipling's ashes were brought to Westminster Abbey to lay in Poets' Corner on January 23rd 1936, as George V's body was brought to London to lie in state at Westminster Hall.

'The King is dead,' the papers said, 'and has taken his trumpeter with him.'

SUMMARY

Kipling's last book, the autobiographical *Something of Myself*, was published after his death in 1937.

That Kipling was a writer of great genius there is no doubt, a supreme craftsman, who had a massive influence on the lives of millions of people. Undoubtedly the master of the short story and verse he was a phenomenal best seller. No writer since Dickens had made such an impact. He was the author of the common people and unlike any other English writer.

From his early days in India, through his extensive travelling, to his later isolated sombre years at Batemans, Kipling's vivid imaginative writing spanned the whole spectrum of human emotions. Each of his books provoked comment and analysis. His love of children is reflected in the tender, caring way he wrote for them. He was involved with the Boy Scouts and Girl Guides movements. His old friend Baden Powell, the founder, used the wolf packs from Kipling's Jungle Books as a pattern and Kipling himself later became a Commissioner of the movement.

He had his literary critics. Fellow writers were critical of his style and what they called his abuse of dialect. There were aspects about Kipling which made him unpopular with many intellectuals. He was, however, unconcerned by their jibes.

Politically, many people found his imperialist attitude distressing and his extreme right-wing views were despised by many Liberal-minded people.

After the First World War, which he viewed to be a time of missed opportunities, he preached to the nation to prepare for the next conflict. Britain was drained and sick of war. It was unwilling to listen and during the 1920s and 1930s his popularity and influence ebbed. His prophetic views were sadly to come true in 1939 as they had done in 1914.

Despite his inflexible views, Kipling had a genuine hope for a peaceful and united world and a desire for the happiness of the ordinary man. He feared the worst horrors would occur in Europe if the British Empire was incapable of preventing it.

It is said that behind every great man there is a woman and his beloved Carrie truly bears out this statement. His reliance on her was great, her loyalty was unbending. Among many other duties, she attended to his business matters, ensured he received his privacy when writing and arranged the entertaining at Batemans. She was the refuge he could always turn to in times of trouble. Her resolve at the time of the death of their daughter Josephine was inspirational.

In 1939 when Carrie Kipling died she left Batemans to the National Trust as a memorial to her husband. The Trust has meticulously maintained Batemans through the years and the visitor today can view it as Kipling would have left it in 1936. The watermill has been restored to full working order. Also on show is the Rolls-Royce owned by Kipling between 1928 and 1934. A visit to Batemans is a rewarding experience.

One can only be staggered by the number of miles covered and countries visited by Kipling during his life, when travel was not the simple plane-hopping business it is today. He would be away at sea for many months at a time.

After his death his reputation and the sale of his books declined as did the Empire he so passionately believed in. However, during the 1960s his popularity revived and his books are still widely read today.

His works gained still wider acclaim when brought to the cinema screen, probably the most notable being the 1967 Walt Disney cartoon version of *The Jungle Book.* Several other films, including the 1949 version of *Kim,* starring Errol Flynn, were made for the silver screen.

Small in stature Kipling may have been but he was truly great in achievement, and there is little doubt that his name is written indelibly into the annals of literary history.